the
ANGEL
dialogues

Published by Lorimer Press
Davidson, North Carolina

Printed in the U.S.A.

ISBN 978-0-9897885-2-6
Library of Congress Control Number: 2014931469

"In the Hopkins Manner" was first published in *Bay Leaves*,
Poetry Council of NC, 2013.

PRAISE FOR *THE ANGEL DIALOGUES*

I love that the first "spirit guide" in Tony Abbott's new book is no Virgil but a common mouse. And how fitting, since the word muse, for which the poet is desperately searching, is only one letter short of the word mouse. Unlike Dante's Beatrice, the angel who finally shows is a double tasking, sarcastic (You needed me bad), Yeats reading, quantum-leaping trickster. And in spite of her slang and jargon-filled pedagogy (I don't do New York, darling), she leads the poet once again to all he thought he had lost: a deep trust in the creative process and in the art of living, and a gracious acceptance of whatever might fall next from the unpredictable sky.

— *Cathy Smith Bowers*
Poet Laureate of NC 2010-2012

Among all the things I've admired about Tony Abbott's work over the years – and those things are legion – his refusal to flinch or shy away from his spiritual preoccupations intrigues and thrills me most profoundly. His new book, *The Angel Dialogues*, mines with even more profundity and lyric intensity that sacred vein – with an imaginative finesse and sense of humor that is at once mystical and accessible. *The Angel Dialogues* is a book-length suite of poems about a played-out, cynical poet – "the poet who / waits / for the feather to / drop / from the unpredictable / sky." Spiritually fatigued, desperate for that next great poem, he cries out to forces beyond him for help and is visited for the next year by a young iconoclastic woman angel, the angel of our dreams – who, not incidentally, reads Yeats and knew Whitman, and becomes not only his Muse, but his perfect capstone poem. Abbott miters each poem into the next with the precision of a master carpenter, in language that moves seamlessly, often floating, from impressionism into a quirky vernacular narrative that sounds, in its prayerful simplicity, like a ceremony. A beautiful, humane book that takes big stunning chances.

— Joseph Bathanti
Poet Laureate of NC, 2012-

Tony Abbott's angel wears boots and sells girl scout cookies. She watches him write poems, she plays bridge, she hangs around to make sure he doesn't mess things up, and if he does, she still loves him.

"We are the fingers of God's mourning," she tells him in an almost unbearably moving poem about the small victims of the Newtown shootings. At intervals the poet watches the world around him ebb and flow, especially the trees. The trees become the poet, they sing together, and they welcome the shadows together. This book is one of the most emotionally wide-open collections of poetry that I've read in a long time. It spirals between the angel's words and the poet's solitary encounters with the landscape, both inner and outer. This angel is guide, in her hiking boots and field jacket. She knows the lay of the soul's land. Yes, the poet has created her out of his longing – or maybe it's the other way around? As the late Randall Jarrell might say, in the manner of his great poem "Field and Forest," the poem can't tell the two of them apart.

— Kathryn Stripling Byer
Poet Laureate of NC 2005-2009

If I were allowed to choose my angel, I might embrace Gracie, as portrayed in Anthony S. Abbott's *The Angel Dialogues*. Solicitous, assured, understanding, cheeky (Say what?), impudent (!), mischievous(?!), wiseacre(!?!), she is the counselor who does not insist, the consoler who does not impinge; she is the One who will trust me when I cannot trust myself. Like certain other aspects of Nature, she teases us into faith. Thank you, Angel. Thank you, Tony.

— Fred Chappell
Poet Laureate of NC, 1997-2002

the
ANGEL
dialogues

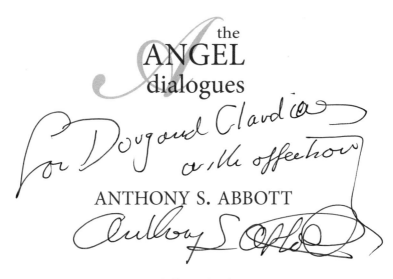

ANTHONY S. ABBOTT

with illustrations by

Betsy Hazelton

for Clara & Josie

THE POET PRAYS FOR A MUSE

"Nothing can come of nothing," he writes.
Overhead, the black masks of the hurricanes
fly by. The TV drones of the day's tragedies,
the stupid sins of the rich and famous.
Not even the cries of the hungry can rouse him.
"I am dying, Egypt, dying," he murmurs.
His head spins like the horses on the carousel,
the horses on their silver poles.
                          For a long time, he sleeps,
his dreams as grey as the clouds that children draw,
slipping, sliding outside their preplanned lines,
dreams like the spaghetti straps of torn dresses,
like red taillights disappearing in the mounting fog.

He wakes exhausted, wakes and sleeps again.
Sometimes at night he dozes on the screen
porch, listening to the almost silent march
of the rain. He prays for help.

One morning, curiously, he sees a mouse
near the front door, waiting it seems, to be
let out. He opens the door to blue sky
and the scent of gardenias down the hill.
He follows the mouse out into the day.

THE ANGEL ARRIVES

When the angel came to me
under the streetlight
I was afraid and hid my eyes
from her strange brightness

so she took my hand and led
me through the dark streets
till we came to a path
in a white bark wood

and I reached for her
but she was only air.

THIS ANGEL STUFF

We are sitting on a bridge over a stream
in a birch wood. The angel is on my left.
She dangles her bare feet over the side.
She turns and looks at me. *Don't be afraid,*
she says.

       "This is a dream, it must be a dream,"
I say. *No,* she says. Her voice is like
the evening star after sunset. It holds the night.

"Who are you?"
Your angel, she says.
"My angel?"
Yes, your very own.
"How?'
 Her laughter is a tiny bell, a glass bell.
Don't ask how. I just am. That's all.
"That's a lot."
Yes, she says. *Anyway, you asked for me.*
Over and over you asked for me, didn't you?
"Yes, but I didn't expect anything like this."
What did you expect?
"A voice, I guess. A spirit. Something vague
and mysterious. The rustling of leaves. I don't know."
You humans, she says. *The rustling of leaves, indeed.*
You have no imagination.

"Raphael," I say. "Your hair."
She smiles and runs her fingers
through her auburn curls.
That's better, she says.

I turn and look at her.
I try to speak, but nothing comes out.

You all do that, she says, *until you get used
to us. Just relax. Be happy. We have
a lot of work to do.*
"This angel stuff," I say, "is pretty amazing."
It is, indeed, she says, and vanishes.

ANGELS IN THE TREES

In the trees above the streetlight
angels swarm like bees.
"Can they come down?" I ask.
No, my angel says, *Only me.*
"Why?"
Those are the rules, you only get one.
"And I have you."
Yes.
"I'm glad, I wouldn't want anyone else."
Any angel else.
"No. I mean yes. No angel else."
You're funny, she says.

I look up at the throng.
"What are they doing?" I ask.
Listening.
"Listening to what?"
To you, silly, to all of you.
How do you think we know where
to go? We listen. You talk to us,
you pray, you tell us what you need.
We listen, then we go.

"You can hear everybody, everything?"
Sort of, but not really.
Too much interference. Too many
talking at the same time. But we make
it out. You were easy.
"I was?"
Those poems, you know, those terrible
poems about aging, about dying. You
needed me bad.
"You read my poems?"
I watched you write them.
"Oh."
You have to trust me.
"What?"
Don't worry about what I know
or don't know. Just trust me.
"I'm scared."
I know. Too much all at once.
Just trust me. O.K.?

I stammer out something. And she's gone.

THE ANGEL READS YEATS IN THE LIBRARY

Monday morning, before ten.
I'm in the stacks, in the 828's.
I turn the corner at the Y's.
There she is, sitting cross legged
reading Yeats. *He's really good*, she says
without even looking up. She pats the floor.
Come, sit down next to me, she says.
I start. *No, the other way*, she laughs,
so I can see your face. I place
my back against the M's—Milton.
She faces me. I can see her bare feet.
"Aren't you cold?" I ask.

What? she asks, looking up.
Oh that, she laughs. *They all ask
about that. The answer is 'no.'
We don't feel hot and cold. Now
listen to this*, she says:
'*How but in custom and in ceremony
Are innocence and beauty born?
Ceremony's a name for the rich horn
And custom for the spreading laurel tree.*'

"It's very beautiful," I say. *A Prayer
for My Daughter*, she says.
"I know."
*OK. If you know so much, tell me
what it means.*

"You tell me—you're the angel."

I never did quite understand Willie.

"Don't be ridiculous. Just tell me,

in your own angelic words, what it means."

No, Professor, you tell me.

THE ANGEL WATCHES ME WRITE

"You distract me," I say.

You wanted a Muse, didn't you?

"Yes, but. . ."

You prayed for a Muse.

"Yes."

And you got me.

"I know, but…"

But what?

"It makes me nervous when. . ."

I stand behind you and look over your shoulder?

"Yes."

I need to see what you're writing.

"But you're an angel. Don't you just
know? Can't you see from wherever. . ."

No, sweetheart, I can't.

"Can't you just come back and read it
when I'm done? I'll read it out loud to you."

But why, sweetheart? Don't you want me here?

"Of course I do. I always want you here."

Except when you're writing.
"Except when I'm writing."
But I'm your Muse. If I go away
you won't have anything to write about.
"Oh come on. You can Muse me from
wherever…"
You don't know that. You don't even
know where wherever is.
"Well, you could be invisible, then,
and give me little voice hints."
It doesn't work like that.
You need my presence, my
what-do-you-call it. . .my aura.
"Oh," I say. I place my fingers
on the keys. Words appear.

THE FALL

The October sun
mocks me

with its noise,
slanting

across the turning
earth

in yellow
lines.

The wild geese
fly south

their bellies gold
from the early

morning light.
You

are not
here.

THE ANGEL ATTENDS A FELLOWSHIP SUPPER

"Introduce me to your friend," says the man
across the table. I didn't know I had a friend.
I turn and look. "Oh Lord," I say. It's the angel.
"Where did you get that hat?" I whisper.
It's a kind of inverted basket with dried
flowers.

      In the clothes closet, she laughs
and touches the hat with her hand. Something
falls into her mashed potatoes. Her dress looks awful.
"I suppose you got that from the clothes closet,
too," I say.

             "What's that?" asks the man,
who is fortunately a bit hard of hearing. He
has curly white hairs growing out of his ears.
Penelope Harrington, smiles the angel,
and extends her hand. They shake. He recoils.
"My goodness, Penelope," he says. "I felt
an electric shock. *Indeed,* says Penelope,
I sometimes affect people that way.
She gives him her full dimpled smile.
"What are you up to?" I hiss.

                   "Archibald
McDonald," he says, and smiles back.
He's one of those old missionaries, high
pants and suspenders, shirt buttoned
at the neck, no tie. "Could I get you some
dessert, Penelope?"

"Ladies room,"
I whisper. "Now." She drops her eyes with
great delicacy. *Archibald, dear, would*
you excuse me for a minute. Call of nature,
you know.
      "Me too," I mutter.
We meet in the hall. *Well,* she smiles,
how do you like my outfit? Just like
an old trooper.
"This is ridiculous. Why are you here?"
It's part of my training.
"Why?"
They want me to get to know. . .
"Know what?"
The church, silly. God wants me to give
a report on the church. . .I attend different,
you know, . . .functions.
I look down at her feet. Black shoes,
very sensible. "I miss your toes,"
I say. She blushes and goes back
to Archibald, who asks her to play
Bingo on Saturday night in the
retirement home. I'm lost.

THE ANGEL SPEAKS OF BEAUTY

"Are you. . .?"
Am I what?
"Are you, well, beautiful, you know,
up there?"
*Well, of course, I am. Everyone
is beautiful up there.*
"So, you don't just look at someone
the way I look at you and say, 'Wow,
you're beautiful."
No, sweetheart, we don't do that.
"But, why not. . .oh, I know, you're
going to give me the everyone
is equal line, everyone's the same."
Well, then, darling, why ask?
"Because, here it's so hard
for people who are not beautiful.
They look at themselves and feel sad.
What do you say to people
who feel they aren't beautiful?"
I love you, she says.
"I know you do."
*No, silly, you tell the unbeautiful ones
you love them.*

"But suppose you don't. Suppose
their ugliness puts you off."
Get over it. All the more
reason to love them.
"But if you can't."
You can. If you can't, then what
am I doing here? Don't you see,
darling? Don't you see why I'm
here? Look at me, sweetheart.

I look at her, and start to cry.
Yes, she says. *You know. Now*
just go love everyone like that,
and then they'll be beautiful,
just like I am.

THE ANGEL SPEAKS OF WRESTLING

She looks terrible, bruises
on her dimpled cheeks.
"Oh my God," I say,
"what happened to you?"
Wrestling, she says.
"With who? With what?"
A wild man. He wouldn't
give up. I had to put his
thigh out of joint, and still
he hung on to me. And he said,
'I will not let you go unless
you bless me.' So I blessed him.
What else could I do?

"Wait a minute," I say. "I know
this story. His name is Jacob."
It was Jacob, she says. *But I changed*
it to Israel.
Yes, and he went away limping, just
like you.
"Right," I say. "He saw the face of God
and lived. He's the last one in the book
who sees the face of God."
Until Jesus, she says.
"Until Jesus," I repeat.

Then she winks at me. *Look*
at me, she says. *I was so beautiful*
before.

POEM IN THE KEY OF E

Some trees keep their color and shape
even beyond the time that we have ceased
to dream. They tease us into faith.

This one I approach from a distance.
Its leaves, like tiny flags of grace,
beckon to me. It is November, and the rain

has pelted us, sweeping masses
of yellow to the sodden earth.
But these leaves stay, and the tree,

bright orange against the now blue
sky, stands against the growing dark.
Some days I am afraid to come,

fearing that a mean and fickle God
will flip the table, leaving me nothing
but a tangle of dark and dirty branches.

The neighbors think I'm weird.
"For Christ's sake," the plumber says.
"It's just a fucking tree." Maybe.

I thought that once myself. But now
if I close my eyes hard in the night,
the color comes and the room

slides away. I float upward in this
orange, this strange treeness.
My body is inside, looking out.

THE ANGEL SPEAKS OF HEAVEN

"So," I ask, "When you're not here,
where are you?"
Heaven.
"Ah."
Ah, what?
"Aha!"
What?
"I gotcha."
Explain yourself, darling.
"Heaven exists."
Of course it does.
"It's a real place."
Yes.

"Well, what do you do there?"
We sing hymns and flap our wings.
"What wings?"
*The wings you earn, like that movie
everyone watches at Christmastime.*
"And you?"
*I take care of people like you.
I wrestle, I make announcements.*
"And in heaven, you just sing?"
Yes.
"Pretty boring."
*That's what Mark Twain said.
I liked him. He was a real wise-ass.*
"You don't just sing."
*Of course, not, sweetheart. Come on,
use your imagination.*

"What do you do?"

We talk about you.

"Me?"

Not just you. Everyone.

"But there are so many of us, millions

and millions of us."

We don't have time.

"Of course not, you're too busy."

No, no, no. That's not what I mean.

I mean there is no such thing as time.

Time is a human invention.

Time is death walking.

Where did that come from?

"I'm supposed to be a poet, aren't I?

I mean, you're the one who touched my lips."

That was good, sweetheart. Do

me another one.

"Heaven is the prodigal come home,

kissing the father. Time is the elder

brother, upstairs."

Now, you're rolling.

"Heaven is the blue egg

in the wren's nest. Time is the tornado

touching down in the sweat-worn streets."

Sweet Jesus, darling, you've got it.

THE ANGEL COMES TO THE CHRISTMAS PARTY

When the lights go out she taps
me on the shoulder. *Pretty cool,
huh?* she says affecting that
teenage voice she thinks is funny.
"Christ! What have you done?"
*You were bored. I could tell.
You should see yourself, pacing
from room to room. You look so
silly.*
"Nobody noticed. They're all
too busy yacking. Bla, bla, bla."
*I like that. What's that mean,
that bla, bla, bla?*
"Well, it means a whole lot of
talk about nothing."
Good, then. I was right.

People are lighting candles. Someone
has gone to check the fuse box.
I love the way she looks, sitting
on the chandelier, swinging her ankles.

"Come down," I whisper.
No, she teases.
"Come on. Please?"

The lights come on, extra bright.
"Jesus," says a bearded man.

Now I really have them going,
says the angel. But where is she?
She's playing hide-and-seek.

I find her in the guest bedroom
trying on someone's fur coat,
her beautiful red hair flowing
over the shoulders. She's smiling.
"You are so vain," I say.
Indeed, she says, and then she's
gone. Her aura lingers like the smell
of incense and pine in the summer woods.
The whole house glows. No one knows why.

WHAT THE ANGEL REALLY SAID

"You stink," I say to the angel.
I know, she says. *It's those shepherds.*
Have you ever spent any time around sheep?
Good grief, sweetheart, they are rank.

"But why? I mean how?"
Come on, you know.
Then I get it. "Jesus Christ!" I say.
You might say so.
"You were the one that...."
The one who, sweetheart, mind your grammar.
Here is what I really said.
"But the book!"
The book. The book, she says. *Now*
sit down and listen!

> *Hi guys. I am an angel. I know that sounds*
> *really weird to you. Don't roll your eyes*
> *like that. I could have worn something a little*
> *more modern, but God said—God said, 'Wear*
> *the usual angel garb.' So here I am.*
>
> *Please, please, don't walk away like that.*
> *I have something very special to tell you,*
> *something that will change your lives.*
> *Please, please come back. That's better. Yes,*
> *that's much better. Let's all sit down. OK,*
> *in a circle. Oh, that's lovely. I love circles.*

Now listen. Over in the next town, there is
a girl who's about to have a baby, and that
baby is the son of God. No, no, no, that's
not crazy, it's true. Look here, guys. We don't
really know what God looks like. We don't really
know much of anything about God. And God
doesn't like that. God wants us to know him,
and once we know him, we will love him. So
he is going to be born as a baby, as the son
of this girl in the next town, and he will grow up
and come here to this field and he will speak to you
and to everyone….What? 'Nobody speaks to us,'
you say. That's the whole point. This baby, this man,

this God living in a human body, will speak to you
like nobody else ever has. This God is here for you,
not for the Kings and the Priests, but for you guys
out here on this cold night freezing your buns off.
Now go, find that baby and kneel down and thank
God, over and over again, for bringing that baby
to us.
What? 'Who will take care of the sheep?' I'll tell
you what. If you go right now, and don't stay
too long, I will. Give me one of those crooks.
Oh yes. I forgot. In the barn behind the tavern.
Yeah, in case you have trouble, it's the one
with the big star over it. Now, for Christ's sake,
get going.

THE ANGEL MOURNS FOR THE CHILDREN

It is a week after the children died
and the angel comes to me on the dark path.
We walk in silence to the bridge.
For a long time we sit without speaking.
The eyes of the angel are swollen.

Then she begins. *Emilie*, she says.
 Daniel, Olivia, Josephine, Ana, Dylan,
Madeline, Catherine, Chase, Jesse,
James, Grace, Charlotte, Jack, Noah."

"Caroline," I say, "Jessica, Avielle,
Benjamin, Allison."

All we can do is to name them,
she says. *Every day we name them*
they are still alive in our hearts.

"And God?" I said.
Ah God, the angel says.
God didn't save his own son.
God mourns as we do.

"And you? Do you mourn, too?"

We are the fingers of God's mourning.
We touch the hands of the mothers,
we are the scarves on the necks of the fathers.
We walk on the grass of the graves
and whisper solace to the sisters.

"And I?"

And you, she says, *give the cracked*
cup of your heart to those who need you.
Bless the sun and the swift flying birds
and the crescent of the new moon.

CHINESE PISTACHE

For a long time
        her leaves keep their green
                before she eases

into fall so slowly
        I cannot tell until
                one morning as I
climb the hill
        she is a startling
                burnt sienna.

I stand speechless.
        My hand reaches out.
                I pick three branches

and carry them home
        where they stand
                luminous as light itself

in a tall stone vase.
        They burn their way into
                the incandescent heart.

Then the tree is gone,
        her thin limbs invisible
                against the cloak

of the giant cedar
        lurking behind. She has
                narrowed herself

into winter
        into the white hallowed
                mystery of sleep.

THE ANGEL PLAYS IN THE SNOW

The angel looks like a model—bright red
ski hat with her lovely auburn curls
peeking out below. Baby blue jacket,
tight black ski pants and furred boots.
She's been shopping.

We slide downhill on an orange sled
the angel in front, my arms around
her. She screams with joy.

Later, we lie in the snow in the graveyard
and make angel wings. She thinks
it's hilarious. The flakes tickle our noses.

We go from grave to grave
and the angel touches the markers.

Do you see them? she asks.
"No."
Keep looking, she says. *You will.*
The angel seems to fly
from stone to stone,
faster and faster
like the snow itself
and the spirits join her, dancing
dancing into the falling dark.

THE ANGEL TAKES A BRIDGE LESSON

Two clubs, the angel says.
"Is zat Stayman?" her partner asks.
The angel looks at me. She is playing East-West,
I am one of her opponents. I love it.

It is mid-February. Cold as hell outside.
She's wearing a long skirt, boots, a turtle-neck
with a lovely gold cross. She looks at me
over her half glasses.

No, Kenwood, the angel says.
"Vat?" her partner asks.
"I don't know zat convention."

I don't either. She's up to something..
Her partner is a heavy-set woman
with a German accent. She raises her hand
and calls the teacher over.

"Vat is Kenwood?" she asks. The teacher
blinks and the angel smiles. *I'm so sorry,*
she says to the teacher, touching him
on the wrist. He blushes.

"Did you mean, Blackwood?" the teacher asks.
Silly me, the angel says, and smiles.
The teacher is done in. *Of course,*
she whispers softly. *I just can't seem
to remember all these conventions.*

Then she drops her cards. I bend over
to help her pick them up. "You are crazy," I hiss.
Well, of course, darling. You wouldn't
want it any other way, would you?

They bid three No Trump. The angel is
the dummy. She watches her partner play.
She looks around the room. How intent
they all are. *Look at them,* she says
to me. *They think this is so important,*
whether they make two or three, or whether
they sit them down.
"Set them," I say.
Indeed, she says. *You humans amaze me.*
I look at my partner, who seems not to have noticed
the slip. "We humans amaze me, too," I say.

IN THE GARDEN: LATE WINTER

Today I dig holes
for the new plants.

I shovel compost
into the wheelbarrow

and roll it to the holes.
I fill them in

and pack the green
plants into their new

homes. The painter
works in the carport.

The sun slants through
the bare branches.

It is cold. The wrens
have gone south.

PRODIGAL ANGEL

Well, she says to me, *I don't know why
I get all these smelly jobs. Pigs this time.*
I think about pigs. "Oh," I say, "you mean
those swine with the unclean spirits, the ones
who drowned in the sea."

Oh, no, she says, *that was a mess. That
wasn't me. I mean the pigs the prodigal
cared for. The book doesn't tell
the whole story.*
                    I know I'm in for a good one,
so I sit down, and she sits opposite. We hold
hands while she talks.

*It says in the book that he came to himself.
That's good. I like that. But you know
he didn't come to himself by himself. It was
my job to convince him. The book leaves out
that part.*
                    "Tell me more," I say. I love to egg
her on. She smiles. *He was a mess, literally
and figuratively. He could no more get up
and go home than fly to the moon. He's taken
the money, ruined his life, he stinks, and he's
sure his father hates him.*

*Your father loves you, I tell him. He jumps up.
He thinks he's hallucinating. This angel stuff
is weird, darling. You got it pretty quick, but a lot
of them never do believe.*

He's running around
in circles saying 'oh shit,' if you will excuse
my language. And I'm saying calm down,
sweetheart, it's ok. I finally get him to look at me.
'Am I crazy?' he asks. 'No.' 'Am I dead? That's it,
I'm dead, and I'm in heaven and you're—
you're so beautiful.'

And I kiss him on his dirty cheek and whisper
in his ear, 'Go home, sweetheart, your father
loves you. He misses you like hell.
He wants you back so bad. Just go home
and kneel down and put your arms around
his bony legs and say you're sorry. It'll be
all right. I promise you.'

For a while he just looked at me and then
he began to cry. 'O God,' he said, and he fell
on his knees and put his filthy arms around my legs
and I touched his hair, which glowed like gold
in the wind. And then he got up and started home.

"The book doesn't mention the hair," I laugh.
No, she says, *but when he got home,*
the father saw it from a long way off, and he knew.

THE ANGEL SELLS GIRL SCOUT COOKIES

The doorbell rings. I open the door.
Three girls are standing there.
One of them is the angel.
What game is this, I wonder.
"Wanna buy some girl scout cookies?"
they cry in unison.
                              The angel's
on the right. She wears little glasses
and her hair's done up in braids.
"What's your name?" I ask her slyly.
Melissa Ann Carter, she winks.
I'm new in the neighborhood.
I try to trap her. "Where do you live?"
I ask. *Down there*, she says,
pointing vaguely to the south.
"Down there," the others cry in unison,
and start to giggle. I know them.
They've never acted like this before.

The angel offers me a box of thin mints.
"You know I don't eat cookies," I say.
No sir, she chirps, *I don't know that.*
"We don't know that," the other girls
echo. They sound like the girls'
chorus in Gilbert and Sullivan. An adult
waits in the car across the street. She blows
the horn. "Come on, girls," she cries.

Well, Mister, the angel
winks. *How about peanut butter? I know
you love peanut butter.* "Do not!" scream
the other girls.

I buy two thin mints and a peanut
butter. I won't eat them. They're bad for me.

Later, the angel stops me at the streetlight.
She laughs and laughs. *You were so funny,
the other day. You didn't know what to say.*
"How in the heck did you bring that off?" I ask.
*The mother never saw me. Adults almost never
see me.*
"And the girls?" I ask.
They forgot everything afterwards.
"How did you manage that?"
Magic, she says.

THE ANGEL COUNSELS PATIENCE

It means 'endure,' she says.
"What?"
What you don't have.
"What don't I have?"
Patience.
"Oh, that."
No, I'm serious. You want everything
right away.
"I want what I want when I want it."
Very funny, she says. *Don't try and*
distract me. We're talking about patience.
It comes from the Latin word for 'endure'
and you don't endure very well.
"OK, I don't endure very well."
You know, I won't always be here.
"I know."
You don't know. You think I don't see you
wandering up and down the streets?
"I'm thinking."
You are not. I know what you're doing.
"What?"
Looking for me.
"If you want me again look for me under your boot-soles."
Whitman. Good. I knew him. He had the same
problem as you, but he learned patience.

Look at the grass. My God. Look at the leaves
on the trees. Turn each leaf over in your hand
and touch it with your tongue.

"Look for the penny on the sidewalk
that says luck," I add.
Annie Dillard, the angel says.
"You knew her, too."
They give me the good ones, don't they?
"They sure do."
Love is patient, she says.
"St. Paul," I say.
He was a weird one, the angel says.
"The thorn in the flesh," I say.
Don't get me started on that, she says
and then she's gone.

ON THE MORNING AFTER

the words vanished
tumbling it seems letter
by letter into the green sea

the "l's" and "m's" sinking
into the primeval darkness
even divers do not reach

the newspaper boxes
startlingly empty
the mouths of the reporters

making soundless motions
the computer screen
a dazzling tweetless blue

on that morning after
the sun still shone
in the innocent sky

the heron still stood
one-legged on the
weathered dock

and on a bare branch
of the highest pine
the hummingbird kept watch.

THE POET NAMES THE ANGEL

Spring night. Azaleas shining, red and white,
in the pale gleam of the full moon. I step outside.
She is sitting on the hood of my car
across the street, painting her toenails.

"Lets walk," I say, "I've got something
serious to ask you."
Just a minute, she says, and blows on her toes.
I wait, and then I wait some more.
I don't think this is my color, she says.
We walk. I watch her toes and think.

I take a deep breath. "Do you have a name?"
She blushes, and she says nothing.
"I want to call you by name. Do you have a name?"
No," she says. *Not really.*
"Why not? Doesn't God name you?"
*Oh no, our people name us. Each one
names us,* she says, and she starts to cry.
"Why are you crying," I ask.
The names, the names, the names—
*"Each name brings back the person. This angel
business is hard, sweetheart. I have all these
people. I love them all. I help them all. A little
girl in Venezuela named me Rosalita? Isn't
that marvelous? The angel Rosalita.*
A game strikes my fancy.

"France," I say.
Antoinette, she says.
"Russia," I say.
Masha, she says. *It must be Masha.*

"German," I laugh.
Oh God, German. Ilkedoodle.
"The angel Ilkedoodle." We laugh together.

I'm standing under the angel tree. It is empty.
She sits at my feet, yoga style,
and looks up at me. *Well*, she says.
Any ideas?
"I don't know. I don't think I can do this."
Yes, you can. Try. You'll find it.
You always do, eventually.

I close my eyes. Then I know.
"Grace," I say. "Gracie," "Gracia."
Indeed, she says, and floats upward
into the leaves.

THE ANGEL SPEAKS OF EMILY DICKINSON

Of course I knew her. How could I not know her?
Gracie laughs and shows her dimples. When she laughs
the sky turns pink in the west. We are walking
along the lake shore.

"She didn't like God very much," I say.
No, she didn't.
"And how did God feel about that?"
God sent me to her.
"You're kidding."
Where do you think all those poems came from?
"From her imagination!"
Gracie laughs again, and the sky
turns orange.

I was there, in that room, in the window, on the bedpost.
Without me she might have given up, you know. God
is no dummy. He understands these things.
'Write them and put them away,' I said to her.
Your barefoot rank is better.

"Come on, Gracie," I say. "You're making this up. Those are her words."
But where did she get them ? 'Tell the truth, but tell it slant,
My business is circumference.'

"You're kidding me," I say.
Yes, darling, I'm kidding you. Don't be so serious.
Let's just say I helped. Her beautiful imagination
did the rest. But one thing I really did do:
'Mail the letters out of town,' I told her.
'Then they won't gossip at the Post Office.'
Gracie laughs again. The sky turns dark.
We head for home.

"You're amazing Grace," I say.
Yes, that's a great hymn.

THE WHITE DRESS
At the Emily Dickinson House, Amherst, Mass.

Up the stairs
        the white dress there
                in the front window

and your room, white,
        the small bed and bureau,
                a table and chair

You appear—your red hair,
        red hair and the smile
                impish, roguish

you in the white dress
        smiling as if to say
                All these years

you've got me wrong—
        stop bowing and think
                of me now with my

incandescent smile
        and my rueful laugh
                at life's absurdities.

Here I am in my
        white dress at the top
                of the stairs.

That's as far as I will go.

THE ANGEL AND THE BED POST

I see her in the tree above the lamp post
with the other angels.
They are murmuring like the wind.
The leaves are shaking.
Then they are gone, and she
is with me on the street.

"Where did they go?" I ask
I don't know, she says. *Hurricanes, floods,*
volcanoes erupting. I get to stay.
"Yes," I say, "Thank you, Gracie. I need you."
I know, she says. *You've been away*
a long time.
"It's my leg," I say. "I couldn't walk.
I couldn't get down here. I couldn't find you."
I know, she says. *I was watching you.*
"But, if you were watching. . ."
Then why didn't I appear to you?
"Exactly."

She puts her arm in mine, and we walk slowly.
I am still not well, but I am better.

You know, she says, *we angels don't really*
have bodies. We are. . .
"Disembodied sprits," I say. "I've done some reading."
Indeed, she laughs. *In your house, you can't see me.*
But I am there, standing by your bed post, watching you.
"Really? Oh my goodness, I love that."
I turn and look her in the eye. "I really love that."

Yes, she says. *I come as a spirit, I come as the wind,*
as the glint of the moon through the window."
"Very poetic, darling."
I do my best. You're the word person, I hear.
"I do my best."

When I am with her, my leg doesn't hurt. I don't
even know I have a leg. I just walk. We hold hands.

I'm always with you. I hear your pain
in the night, I watch you turning and turning.
I know how you hurt, my darling. I can't stop
the hurt, but I can make it less.
That's what we do, we angels, we heal. And you,
my precious one, will heal. But you must be calm,
you must let peace find you.

"Yes," I say. And she is gone, with the other angels
I guess, off to help hurricane victims.

I am alone, outside my door, watching the azaleas
bloom and the dogwoods on this early April morning.

THE ANGEL PLAYS THERAPIST

Water, she says. "Sandy," I reply.
Why Sandy? She looks puzzled.
"The hurricane," I say.
But, why? she asks.
"The water," I say. "The reporter
wading the streets of Hoboken. The people
bunched in the upper windows
looking down into the streets. The black
water everywhere. The houses
on the Jersey Shore crushed
by the coming tide."
You're on a roll, she says.
And how does this make you feel,
all this water
(in her therapist voice)
"Guilty," I say.
Why?
"Because."
Because why?
"You know."
I know. But you have to tell me.
"I do nothing."
Why?
"I don't know. I think of these people
who travel all the way to Russia, to China,
to I don't know where to adopt an orphan."
Yes?
"People who build houses in Honduras,
board by board, brick by brick."

And you?

"I think about it. I send money. I pray."

And?

"And it's not enough."

So?

"I have to do better."

Why don't you?

"I don't know."

That's not enough.

"What do you mean?"

It's not enough of an answer.

You can do better.

"I'm scared."

Scared of what?

"Changing my life."

Why?

"Oh, come on. I'm tired of this."

I know. And we were just getting to the best part.

"What part?"

The part where you open up.

"And say what?"

Hey, I'm the one asking the questions, sweetheart. Now,
you listen. Go home and think about this. Time's up for today.

IN THE HOPKINS MANNER

The crucified Christ hangs on the tired cross.
Bones break with the weight of the weary world.
He shudders once, and the dark ditch of death smiles.

On barren beaches weathermen wipe the flying seafoam
from their eyes. I watch deep, deep into the night.
I cannot take my eyes from the screaming waves,
the red coated reporter in hip deep water.

In my city the fierce wind shrieks. The flying poles
knock on the door of doom. Headless mannikins
float on the flooded streets. On the morning after,

dead leaves stick to the pitted asphalt. The blood
of autumn turns tawny, turns dirty brown.

In the ark the dinosaurs rumble in the mud thick hold.
The ivory Christ rests silently in the tear-torn tomb. I wait.

THE ANGEL SPEAKS OF DISTANCE

For nights I stand under the streetlight
at the usual time, and then at unusual
times. And then at unusual streetlights.
She has changed her ways, I think.
I am trying to outguess her. It's useless.

When she comes, she looks angry.
You're a fool, she says. *Jesus*
was right about you guys.
"Be more specific."
O ye of little faith, she says.

I notice smudges on her face, dirt under her fingernails.
"So where have you been this time?" I ask.
Oklahoma.
"Why?"
Dust.
"Oh," I say. I try to imagine her
swirling in all that dirt.

Listen, she says. *You are going about this*
all wrong. You've got to stop looking for me.
Just live your life. I keep telling you that.
"But you're more interesting."
Of course I am. But I'm just temporary.
You know that don't you?
"I don't like it."
But you know it.

There is a long silence.
The silence of distances, she says. *You*
can't control that, you know. You can't
control anything. We come when we come.
It's a gift. And she's gone....

The silence of distances. Dust on the paved road.
I walk home.

THE ANGEL RETURNS FROM BOSTON

"Were you there?" I ask her.
She will not speak to me. She stands
in the center of the labyrinth, her toes
on the edge of the inmost circle.
Follow the path, she says to me.
I must come to her by the turns. I must not
cross the lines. *Slowly,* she says.
Do not hurry your steps. With each step,
pray for a person, pray for life, pray
for the coming of the sun from under
the smudge of death.
I pray. I come to the center, then turn
and follow her out.

You know we cannot interfere, darling.
We can only give patience to the wounded.
We can only try and heal the heart.

"Yes," I say. "You are the comforter."
One of them, she says.
"The best," I say.

And then I think of the man who used
his belt for a tourniquet, tied it tight
around the leg of the woman named
Roseann, then disappeared. He never showed
himself again. "Was that you?" I ask her.
It doesn't matter, she says. *When people do*
what's right, who cares what makes it happen?

"I do," I say.
Yes, I know you do. That's your problem.

THE ANGEL THINKS OF MUSIC

We are sitting by the lake. May. Early morning.
Mist rising. I feel brave.

"What is God like?" I ask.
God is like music, she says. Her words startle me.
"How can that be?" I ask.
Think of it, she says. *Music is the most beautiful of all
human endeavors. Music is language without words.*
"So is painting," I say, "or sculpture."
But it's not the same, she whispers softly. *Music
is never only of itself. It is the other world made manifest.*

"How is that?"
For a moment she is silent. Then she speaks.
Close your eyes. Take your very favorite piece of music."
"Mozart," I say. "Piano Concerto No. 21, Second Movement."
Adagio, she says. *Now play the notes in your head. Every note.
One at a time. Hear them in your inner ear. Can you do that?*
"Yes," I say. I play the notes to my own piano in my own ear.
Every note, one at a time.

I count the notes in my high mind. Each finger a world,
each note black or white perfect in the moment,
then gone. Tears come like rain
after long drought. Like the smell of hibiscus
on a distant branch. The sun rising,

God's touch as the day begins.

NEW YORK ANGEL

"I've been in New York," I say.
I know, she answers.
"I met an angel at LaGuardia Airport."
I know.
"His name was Leslie," we both say at once.

"How do you know all this?" I ask.
Leslie is a friend of mine. I asked him
to keep an eye on you.
"Why don't you keep an eye on me?"
I don't do New York, darling.
Leslie does New York. You know, older black man,
some facial growth, nice smile. He likes that look.

"He took me on the M60 bus," I say. "All the way
to Manhattan. Showed me how to take
the subway downtown. I didn't know there was an M60 bus.
I needed five quarters, senior fare,
and I had only three. He gave me the other two."

He said you were nervous.
"I was. He told me to watch my bag
and keep my hand on my wallet. Said he lived
in Miami and came to New York once a month
on business."

He likes that story, the angel says. I*t puts
people like you at ease, makes them feel better.*

"Maybe he wasn't an angel," I say. "Maybe he
was a real human being. Maybe that was
his real life."

Maybe it was, the angel says.
"Like the man in Boston with the belt," I say.
Right, the angel says.
"Makes no difference," I say.
Now you're getting it, she says, and off she goes again.

THE ANGEL SPEAKS OF DEATH

It's really death, she says.
I wince at the word.
It's really death you're afraid of.
"Yes," I say.
Get over it, she says.

We are walking in the white bark wood. She stops
and turns to face me. I look into her eyes.

Death's nothing, she says.
"That's the point," I answer.
What do you mean?
"It's the nothing I'm afraid of."
Ah, she says. *Go on.*
"The absolute emptiness of it. The loss of everything. All the words,
all the beautiful words, the moments, the flow of the ocean,
the white majesty of the shifting stars, all saved in the mind,
all swept into patterns of beauty. The flower on the bedside
table after the accident….All lost, all without a mark.
No mind, no words, no sight, no touch, no scent."

Nice job, she says and smiles her unearthly smile.
Now do some more.
"Wait a minute," I say. "This is a trick. You're an angel. You know
about this. You must know about this. Why should I talk?
Tell me, my angel, tell me about death. Am I wrong?
Oh God, how I'd like to be wrong. I just can't get that
emptiness, that nothing out of my head."

We are sitting now, on the bridge, our feet dangling.
I don't know how we got here, when we sat. I look
into the water, and wait.

I can't tell you, she says. *I'm not allowed.*
"Not allowed! What kind of answer is that?"
The truth, she says. *It's not part of who we are.*
Don't be angry, sweetheart, she says. *That doesn't help.*

"Not part of who we are," I murmur.
The dogwood in the spring, she whispers, *just is,*
it does not think about its isness.

"Its isness," I laugh. "Where on earth did you get that?"
I made it up, she says. *Just be,* she says softly.
Don't worry. Let God worry for you.

And she kisses me once on the cheek, and then the wood
and the stream are gone and I am alone on the dark street.

UNEXPECTED

The bird of the world folds
her wings

and perches on the tree
of night

the owl sleeps with one
eye open

like the poet who
waits

for the feather to
drop

from the unpredictable
sky

ACKNOWLEDGEMENTS

The Angel Dialogues is different from my other poetry collections. With the exception of "In the Hopkins Manner," which was published by the N.C. Poetry Council in *Bay Leaves* (2013), none of these poems has been previously published. This book is not really a collection of poems; rather, it is a narrative, a story that takes place over a year, in which a poet, who has prayed for a muse, receives instead an angel who teaches him much about what it means to be a human being, and leaves him, at the end of that time, wiser, healthier, and more spiritually aware.

I owe a great debit of gratitude for to many people for their help during the writing of this book: to Leslie Rindoks at Lorimer Press for her faith in the book and her beautiful design, to Betsy Hazelton for her marvelous illustrations of the angel in her sundry disguises, to Allison Elrod for her excellent editing skill. To Malaika King Albrecht, Ann Campanella, Barbara Conrad, Dannye Romine Powell, and Beth Swann for their reading of the manuscript and their suggestions for changes and improvements.

Anthony S. Abbott
Davidson, NC.
November, 2013

Anthony S. Abbott is the Charles A. Dana Professor Emeritus of English at Davidson College where he served as Department Chair from 1989 to 1996. He is the author of four critical studies, two novels and six books of poetry, including the Pulitzer nominated *The Girl in the Yellow Raincoat*. His awards include the Novello Literary Award for *Leaving Maggie Hope* (2003), the Oscar Arnold Young Award for *The Man Who* (2005), and the Brockman-Campbell Award for *If Words Could Save Us* (2011) as well as the Irene Blair Honeycutt Award for Lifetime Achievement in the Arts. He lives in Davidson, North Carolina with his wife, Susan.